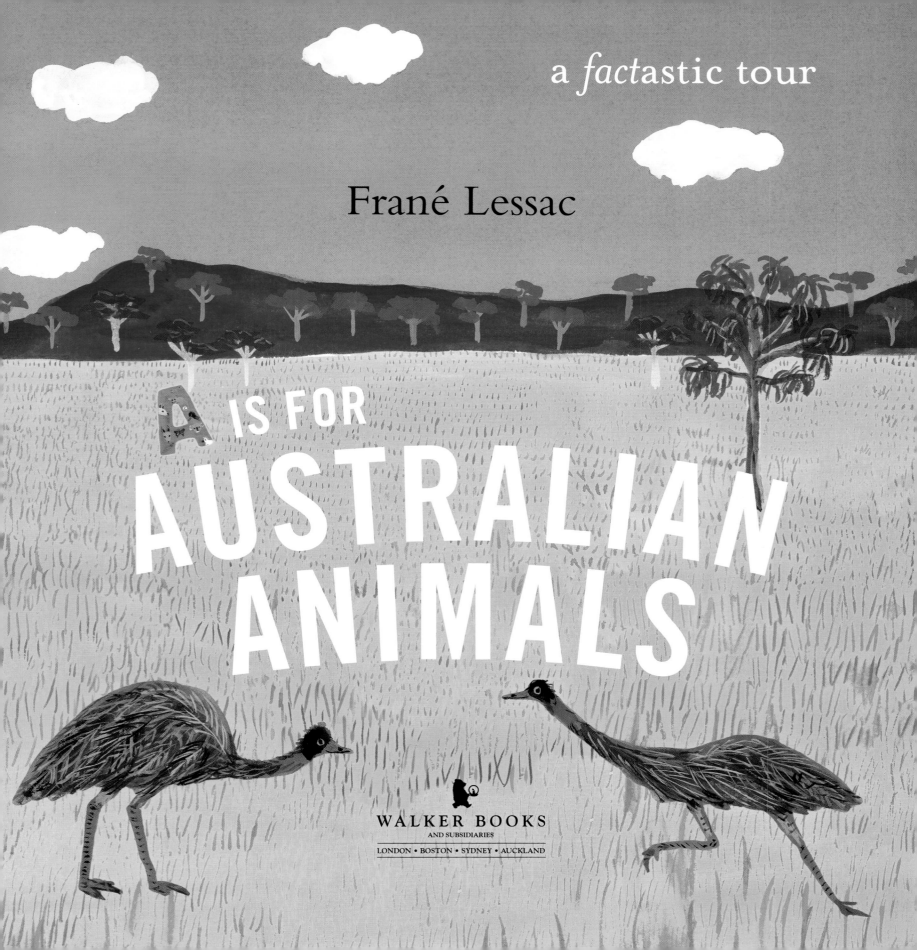

a *factastic* tour

Frané Lessac

A IS FOR
AUSTRALIAN
ANIMALS

WALKER BOOKS
AND SUBSIDIARIES
LONDON · BOSTON · SYDNEY · AUCKLAND

 **Australia** is full of the most amazing animals. Many of them are found nowhere else in the world. From gliding and dancing animals to slithering and hopping ones – all are unique!

This is Christmas Island. It is located in the Indian Ocean, approximately 1565 kilometres from the mainland of Australia.

Australia's isolation has led to the evolution of many strange and wonderful animals.

Australia is a wonderland of birds that are found nowhere else on the globe.

Half of Australia's mammals are marsupials. Marsupial young are born before being fully developed and continue to grow in their mothers' pouches.

Watch where you step! Australia has many snakes, including some of the world's most venomous.

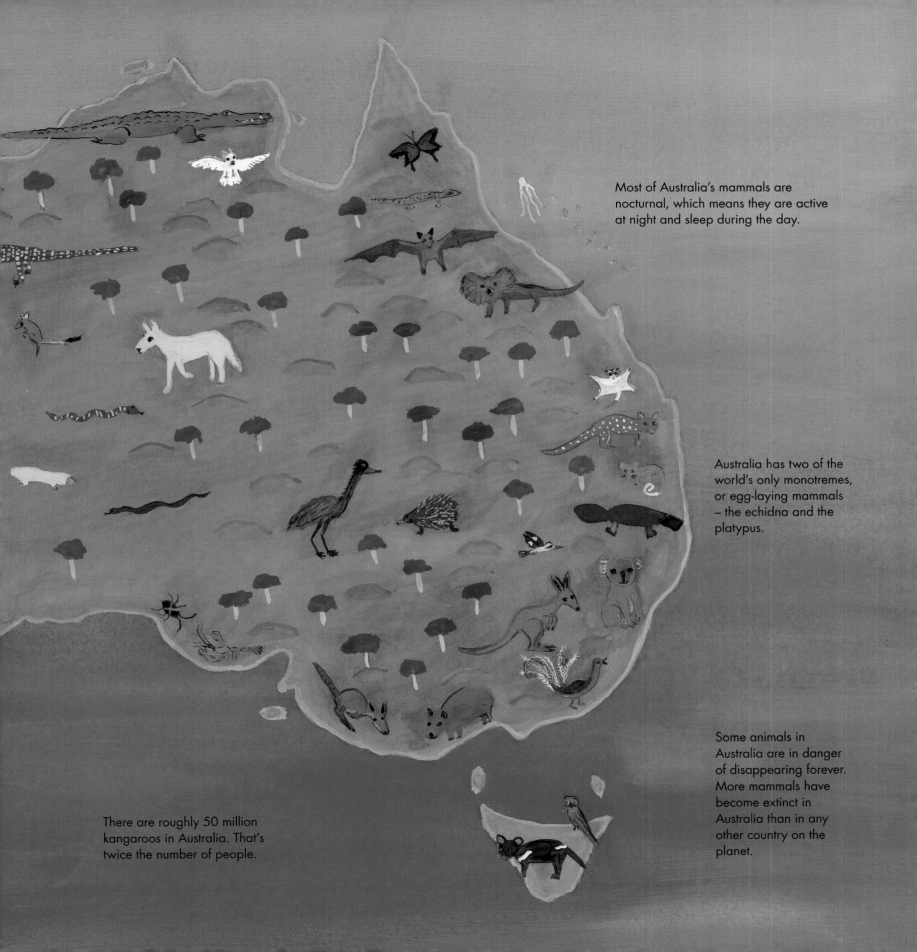

Most of Australia's mammals are nocturnal, which means they are active at night and sleep during the day.

Australia has two of the world's only monotremes, or egg-laying mammals – the echidna and the platypus.

Some animals in Australia are in danger of disappearing forever. More mammals have become extinct in Australia than in any other country on the planet.

There are roughly 50 million kangaroos in Australia. That's twice the number of people.

Bilby

The bilby is a desert-living marsupial with rabbit-like ears.

The desert is a thirsty place. Luckily, bilbies don't need to drink very often. They get water from their favourite foods, like the bush onion, which grows in the sand.

Bilbies don't hop like a rabbit or jump like a kangaroo — they gallop like a pony.

Female bilbies have a pouch that opens backwards. This stops dirt getting into the pouch when the mother digs to find food or to make a burrow.

To escape the heat and predators, bilbies live in spiralling burrows up to two metres deep.

Blue-tongue Lizard

The blue-tongue is a lizard which, if threatened, puffs up its body, opens its mouth wide and sticks out its dark blue tongue.

Lizards, including the blue-tongue, do not produce any body heat. To get warm, they sunbake.

The tail of a blue-tongue lizard is fragile and can break off when it is grabbed by a predator. Unlike other lizards, a blue-tongue's tail only partly regrows and will never be as perfect as the original.

This is a Centralian blue-tongue lizard.

Female blue-tongue lizards do not lay eggs. They give birth to live young.

Cockatoo

The cockatoo is a large parrot with a striking crest on the top of its head.

Like all cockatoos, these sulphur-crested cockatoos can show their moods and feelings or signal danger by the angle they raise their crests.

Cockatoos are loudmouths! Their calls can be ear-splitting, making them one of the loudest parrots.

When cockatoos feed on the ground, a few perch in nearby treetops as lookouts. If there's any sign of danger, they will screech out an alarm.

Crocodiles can leap over two metres out of the water to catch their prey in the air.

Crocodile

The saltwater crocodile is the
largest of all living reptiles.

It's dangerous being a baby
crocodile. Many babies
are eaten before their first
birthday by fish, turtles,
goannas or other crocodiles.

Baby crocodiles chirp in their eggs when they
are ready to hatch. This alerts the mother, who
digs them out and gently carries them to the
water's edge in her mouth.

Crocodiles can grow up to six metres in
length and weigh up to one tonne.

A crocodile is able to float with
only its eyes, ears and nostrils
visible, while the rest of its body
remains hidden under water.

Death Adder

The death adder is one of the deadliest land snakes in the world.

This is the desert death adder. To lure prey, it wriggles its tail like a worm. When animals, birds or lizards come closer to have a look, the death adder strikes with lightning speed and injects venom.

Asian sailors first brought dingoes to Australia about 4500 years ago.

Unlike many snakes, death adder babies are born live and slither off soon after birth.

Dingo

The dingo is a wild dog and Australia's largest land predator.

Dingoes do not bark; they moan, snuff and howl.

Dingoes have special wrists that rotate. When hunting, they can use their paws like hands to pick up food.

To see behind them, dingoes can turn their heads nearly right around in each direction, without moving their bodies.

Echidna

The echidna is a monotreme with sharp spines covering its back and sides for protection.

Emus can run as fast as 50 kilometres an hour.

A baby echidna is called a puggle. When it hatches it is the size of a grape.

Echidnas' hind feet look as if they have been put on backwards! But these backwards feet are handy because they help echidnas to push away the dirt when they are burrowing.

When frightened, echidnas roll into a spiky ball, leaving only their sharp spines visible.

Echidnas use their long, sticky tongues to capture their food of choice – termites and ants.

Emu

The emu is Australia's tallest native bird, but it cannot fly because its wings are too small.

Emus have two eyelids. One is used for blinking and the other stops dust and sand from getting into their eyes.

Leave it to Dad! Once the female emu lays her eggs, she has nothing further to do with the raising of her young. The male emu sits on the eggs until the chicks hatch. He doesn't leave the nest to eat or drink.

Emus lay dark green eggs that weigh nearly half a kilogram each – the same weight as a dozen chicken eggs.

Flying Fox

The flying fox is not a fox that flies! It's a huge bat with a wingspan over one metre from tip to tip.

These are grey-headed flying foxes.

To keep cool on hot days, flying foxes use their wings like fans.

Flying foxes live in large groups called camps, where they are born, raised and roost.

Flying foxes hang upside down because their legs are short and skinny, and not strong enough to support them standing.

Excellent night vision allows flying foxes to see in the dark to search for their preferred foods: nectar, pollen and fruit.

Frill-necked Lizard

The frill-necked lizard has a paper-thin frill around its neck.

Frill-necked lizards spend most of their lives high up in trees. The colour of their skin is ideal camouflage against tree bark.

A frill-necked lizard can open and close its frill like an umbrella to frighten predators.

Goanna

The goanna is a very large lizard. It is the only lizard that has a forked tongue.

This is a perentie goanna. It is Australia's largest goanna, often growing over two metres long, and can be found in the desert.

Like snakes, goannas flick their long tongues in and out nonstop to "taste" the air. This special sense is used for hunting for food.

The perentie goanna is like a speed demon as it can run up to 30 kilometres per hour. That makes it one of the fastest lizards in the world.

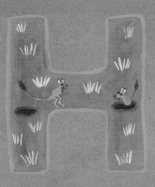

Hopping Mouse

The hopping mouse is a small rodent that jumps like a miniature kangaroo.

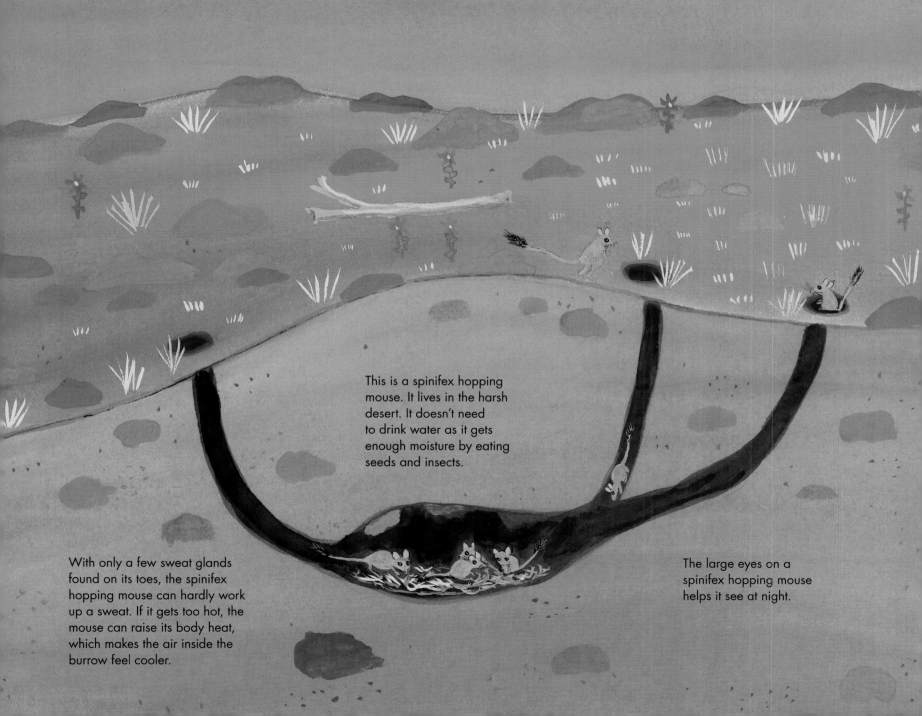

This is a spinifex hopping mouse. It lives in the harsh desert. It doesn't need to drink water as it gets enough moisture by eating seeds and insects.

With only a few sweat glands found on its toes, the spinifex hopping mouse can hardly work up a sweat. If it gets too hot, the mouse can raise its body heat, which makes the air inside the burrow feel cooler.

The large eyes on a spinifex hopping mouse helps it see at night.

Irukandji Jellyfish

The Irukandji jellyfish is one of the most venomous creatures in the world.

Made up of 95 per cent water, Irukandji look like clear jelly, making them difficult to spot.

It is also the smallest jellyfish in the world. Its bell (body) is the size of a human thumbnail.

The Irukandji has deadly stingers on its bell, and tentacles that look like a string of pearls.

An Irukandji sting causes intense pain, cramps, vomiting, headaches and even death if not treated. These symptoms are called Irukandji syndrome.

All jellyfish, including Irukandji jellyfish, have no eyes, ears, nose, heart, bones or brain.

The leatherback turtle is one of the few animals that can eat an Irukandji jellyfish. Luckily, eating the venomous jellyfish doesn't affect the turtle's stomach.

Jumping Spider

The jumping spider is a spider
that pounces on its prey.

These are peacock jumping
spiders. They are about the
size of a small pea.

Jumping spiders, including
peacock jumping spiders, have
eight eyes that look like shiny
beads. The eyes in front include
two large ones that zoom.
Another four eyes on the sides
of their heads give them the
knack of seeing nearly all the
way around.

Some jumping spiders send out vibrations on the edge of a web. This hypnotises its victim to come closer, keep still, or fall asleep while the spider moves in to attack.

Male peacock jumping spiders have black-and-white striped furry legs that they wave like flags to attract females. They also flash their colourful bottom flaps, while performing a dazzling dance.

Peacock jumping spiders do not make webs to catch food. Instead, they hunt.

When a jumping spider jumps, it releases a silk safety rope. If the jump fails, they can use the silk rope to crawl back to safety, just like a rock climber.

Kangaroo

The kangaroo is the largest living marsupial and the largest mammal that hops.

The **kookaburra** has a noisy call that sounds like a human laugh.

Kangaroos turn their ears in all directions to listen for danger. To warn the mob, a kangaroo will thump its feet on the ground.

The long tail on a kangaroo helps it balance when hopping, but the tail is heavy and makes walking backwards nearly impossible.

Kangaroos are born athletes. These eastern grey kangaroos can reach speeds of almost 50 kilometres per hour in a bouncing run and can jump the length of a London bus in a single bound!

Koala

The koala is a marsupial that spends most of its life sound asleep in trees. It sleeps up to twenty hours each day.

Koalas have two thumbs on each of their front paws and one thumb on their back paws. These thumbs give them an expert grip for climbing trees.

The whorls and loops on a koala's fingerprints are almost identical to human fingerprints. Confusing for a detective!

Koalas eat gum leaves that are poisonous to most other animals.

A female kangaroo has muscles that open and close her pouch. She closes the pouch to keep her joey safe, cosy and warm inside, and loosens the muscles to let her joey out.

Lyrebird

The lyrebird is a shy bird that lives in damp forests. It is known for its unique ability to imitate sounds and for its magnificent tail.

In the forest, lyrebirds rake the soil with their long claws to hunt for earthworms, insects and spiders.

Lyrebirds can mimic almost any sound: barking dogs, chainsaws, camera shutters and even car alarms.

Even though the lyrebird has wings, it spends most of the day on the ground. At night-time, it flies up to a tree to roost.

To court a female lyrebird, the male scrapes together a dance floor mound. He then spreads his tail feathers over his head like a shimmery veil, shakes it, struts about and sings.

A male lyrebird's tail of fanned feathers looks like a lyre, an ancient Greek musical instrument.

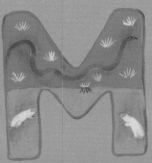

Marsupial Mole

The marsupial mole is a small mammal that lives underground in the sandy desert.

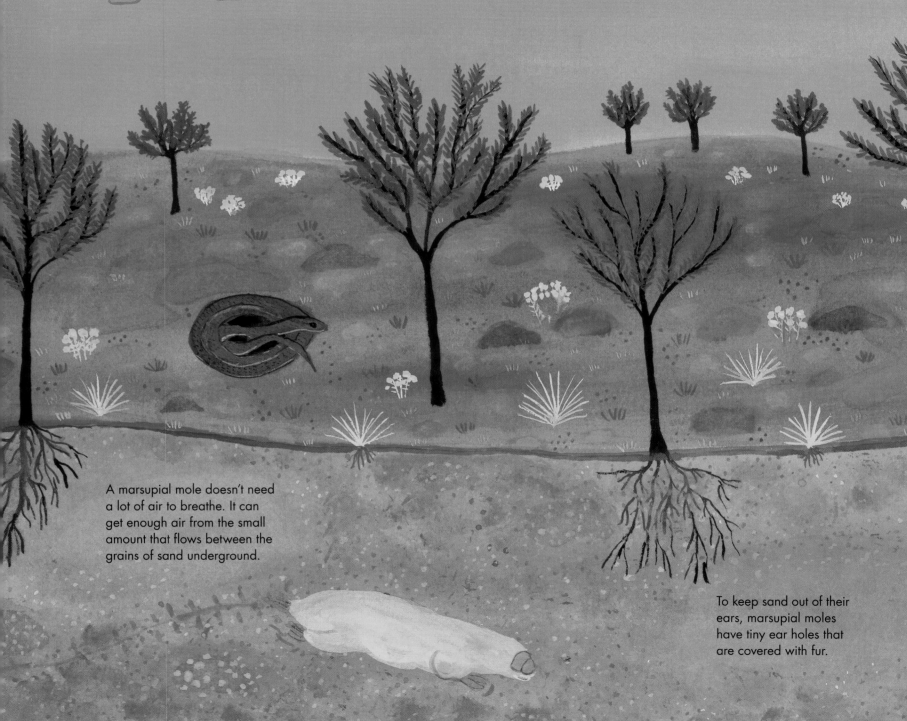

A marsupial mole doesn't need a lot of air to breathe. It can get enough air from the small amount that flows between the grains of sand underground.

To keep sand out of their ears, marsupial moles have tiny ear holes that are covered with fur.

Mulga Snake

The mulga snake, or king brown snake, produces more venom than any other snake.

When mulga snakes bite, they clamp onto their prey and chew, injecting huge amounts of toxic venom.

Like all snakes, the mulga snake hears by picking up vibrations from the ground. It smells by flicking its tongue in and out.

Marsupial moles are blind and use their toughened nose pads and foreheads to bulldoze the sand when burrowing. They also use their spade-like front claws to dig and their back feet to fill in the sand behind them.

Numbat

The numbat is a small marsupial that mostly eats termites.

The colours on a numbat's striped coat provide ideal camouflage in sun-dappled forests.

The female numbat is one of a small number of marsupials that do not have a pouch. A baby numbat must cling tightly to its mother's belly fur.

A numbat has a sensitive nose that can smell termites in the ground. It can feast on up to 20,000 termites a day.

The numbat is one of the few Australian marsupials that is fully active during the day. It hunts in the daytime and sleeps at night in hollow logs or burrows.

A numbat's long sticky tongue is about half the length of its head and body combined.

Oblong Turtle

The oblong turtle has the longest neck of any turtle.

Relatives of the oblong turtle lived on Earth at the same time as dinosaurs.

Oblong turtles have submarine-like skills, including sonar and ballast tanks. These "tanks" are areas in their lungs that can be filled with air or water to control flotation. Because of their long necks, oblong turtles can poke their nostrils above the water's surface, similar to a snorkel.

Baby oblong turtles perform the useful job of snapping up masses of mosquito larvae at mealtimes. This helps to reduce the numbers of annoying mosquitos.

At birth, a hatchling's shell is almost as big as a ten-cent coin. The shell is soft, but hardens once the hatchling starts to eat and bask in the sunshine.

An oblong turtle's snake-like neck is as long as its shell. The neck can be bent and folded sideways under the shell.

Oblong turtles don't have teeth, but they do have very strong jaws. When food swims by, they snatch it with rapid speed. They are so fast they win the award for having the quickest strike of all Australian freshwater turtles.

Platypus

The platypus is a monotreme and one of only a few venomous mammals.

A platypus can find food under water with its eyes and ears closed. It uses its sensitive bill to pick up electric pulses of movement in the water. Playing hide-and-seek would be easy for a platypus!

The double layer of fur on a platypus is denser than the fur of a polar bear. This helps keep it warm and dry in cold water.

The male platypus has poisonous spurs on its back legs.

Possum

The possum is a tree-dwelling marsupial.

When a baby possum outgrows its mother's pouch, it rides piggyback-style on her back.

Ringtail possums build nests in trees out of leaves and grass. The male is the only possum known to help raise its young.

Brush-tailed and ringtail possums have prehensile tails – a tail that can grasp or hold objects. It's like having an extra hand!

Platypuses use webbed feet to swim. On dry land they tuck the webbing under their toes and walk on their knuckles.

Quokka

The quokka is one of the smallest wallabies and the only land mammal on Rottnest Island, off the coast of Western Australia.

Curious and friendly animals, quokkas have grown used to humans visiting Rottnest Island. Posing for a quokka "selfie" is the latest thing for visitors!

Quokkas have a habit of returning to the same area every day to sleep.

Quokkas are able to climb small trees to get food.

An early Dutch explorer thought quokkas were giant rats. He named the island "Rotte nest" ("rats nest"), after them. It later became Rottnest.

Quokkas can get moisture from the plants they eat and can live for months without drinking fresh water.

Unlike other wallabies, quokkas can easily hop about without using their tails for balance.

Red Crab

The red crab migration on Christmas Island, an Australian island in the Indian Ocean, is a world famous event.

Nearly 50 million red crabs live on Christmas Island.

The number of moving red crabs is so big that the people of Christmas Island have built tunnels and bridges to help the crabs safely cross roads.

Each female red crab lays about 100,000 eggs.

At the beginning of the wet season, millions of red crabs migrate from the rainforest to breed and then release their eggs in the sea.

Christmas Island has the largest population of **robber crabs** in the world.

Robber crabs are thieves and have been known to steal silverware, wristwatches, pots and pans, and even sneakers from camp sites.

The robber crab can grow to a gigantic one metre from leg tip to leg tip. It can live up to 60 years.

Sugar Glider*

The sugar glider is a small possum that can glide through the air between forest trees.

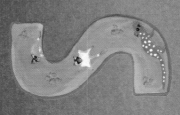

Sugar gliders have a sweet tooth and love eating nectar. They also eat insects and small animals.

Sugar gliders can glide up to 100 metres from tree to tree. That's about the same length as a football field! To glide they use a thin flap of skin that stretches between their wrists and ankles, which acts like a parachute. To steer, they use their tails like a rudder. This is called volplaning.

Adult sugar gliders weigh around 250 grams – about the weight of a large orange.

Spotted-tail Quoll*

The spotted-tail quoll is the largest carnivorous marsupial on the Australian mainland.

* Alphabetical order has been reversed for this page

Spotted-tail quolls are related to the extinct Tasmanian tiger (thylacine).

Spotted-tail quolls are nocturnal, but unlike most marsupials, they come out to sunbake during the day.

When born, spotted-tail quolls are as small as a sunflower seed.

The spotted-tail quoll has a piercing call that sounds like a circular saw.

Sugar gliders nest in tree hollows and rarely visit the ground.

Tasmanian Devil

The Tasmanian devil is the size of a small dog with jaws more powerful than a lion.

Tasmanian devils are at risk from a fatal cancer called Devil Facial Tumour Disease. This disease causes large growths on their faces and necks and other parts of their bodies.

After hearing its terrifying screams and seeing its red ears and sharp scary teeth, early settlers named this animal the Tasmanian devil.

Like a skunk, the Tasmanian devil can squirt a smelly liquid from under its tail when threatened.

In a Tasmanian devil's poo, a wildlife biologist discovered: the head of a tiger snake, an owl's foot, a sock, aluminium foil, half a pencil and the knee of a pair of jeans.

It's hard to spot a Tasmanian devil at night-time. Its black fur helps it to hide from view in the forest.

Tawny Frogmouth

The tawny frogmouth looks like an owl, but is nothing like an owl. It's a nocturnal bird with a frog-shaped mouth.

A tawny frogmouth's feathers are the same colour as bark, making a perfect disguise in trees.

When they close their bright yellow eyes and mouths, tawny frogmouths are almost invisible. When they open their mouths wide, the yellow colour inside attracts insects and moths.

Ulysses Butterfly

The Ulysses butterfly's large blue wings are easy to spot when it's flying.

After this butterfly closes its wings, the black and brown undersides make perfect camouflage for resting or feeding in trees.

The Ulysses butterfly has thousands of lenses in each eye. It is attracted to the colour blue from 30 metres away.

Like other butterflies, Ulysses butterflies don't have noses or lungs. They breathe through little holes on the sides of their bodies called spiracles. They use their feet to taste and smell – talk about table manners!

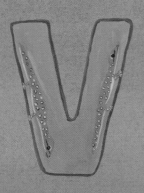

Velvet Gecko

The velvet gecko is a lizard with tiny scales that give its skin a velvety feel.

These are northern-spotted velvet geckos. Like all geckos, velvet geckos have no eyelids, so they cannot blink. They use their tongues to lick their eyes to clean away dirt and dust.

Velvet geckos have microscopic bristles under the pads of their feet that work like velcro. This helps them to climb upside down and along vertical walls.

When a velvet gecko loses its tail, the tail continues to wriggle after being separated from the body. This is painless and a new tail soon grows back. Many geckos will return to eat the tail because it's used to store fat and nutrients when food is scarce.

Wallaby

The wallaby is smaller than the kangaroo, has a shinier coat and its back teeth are flat.

Yellow-footed rock wallabies have sharp claws, thick bushy tails, padded feet and strong hind legs. These all help them bound up vertical rocks and climb tall trees, making them awesome acrobats.

Wallabies that live in rocky areas are called rock wallabies.

Wombats sometimes sleep on their backs with all four feet sticking up in the air.

Wombat

The wombat is the largest burrowing mammal.

Wombats can spend up to two-thirds of their lives in underground burrows. Some burrows are 30 metres long.

Wombat-like creatures have lived in Australia for millions of years.

Wombats produce square poo that they leave on rocks and logs to mark their territory. The flat sides of the poo help keep it in place.

No tooth fairy for wombats. Their front teeth are rootless and keep growing, never wearing away.

If threatened, wombats angle their thick-skinned rear ends at the attacker to protect themselves.

Crusader Bug

The crusader bug is an insect with an x-shaped cross on its back. As there are no Australian animals that start with X, the crusader bug has taken the X spot!

Crusader bug young are called nymphs. Instead of an X on their backs, they have two yellow dots.

There are many cool names for freshwater crayfish across Australia. Some are koonac, gilgie, marron and the red claw.

To escape danger, yabbies propel themselves backwards with a flip of their tail fin.

Yabby

The yabby is a freshwater crayfish found in streams, lakes, dams, rivers and swamps.

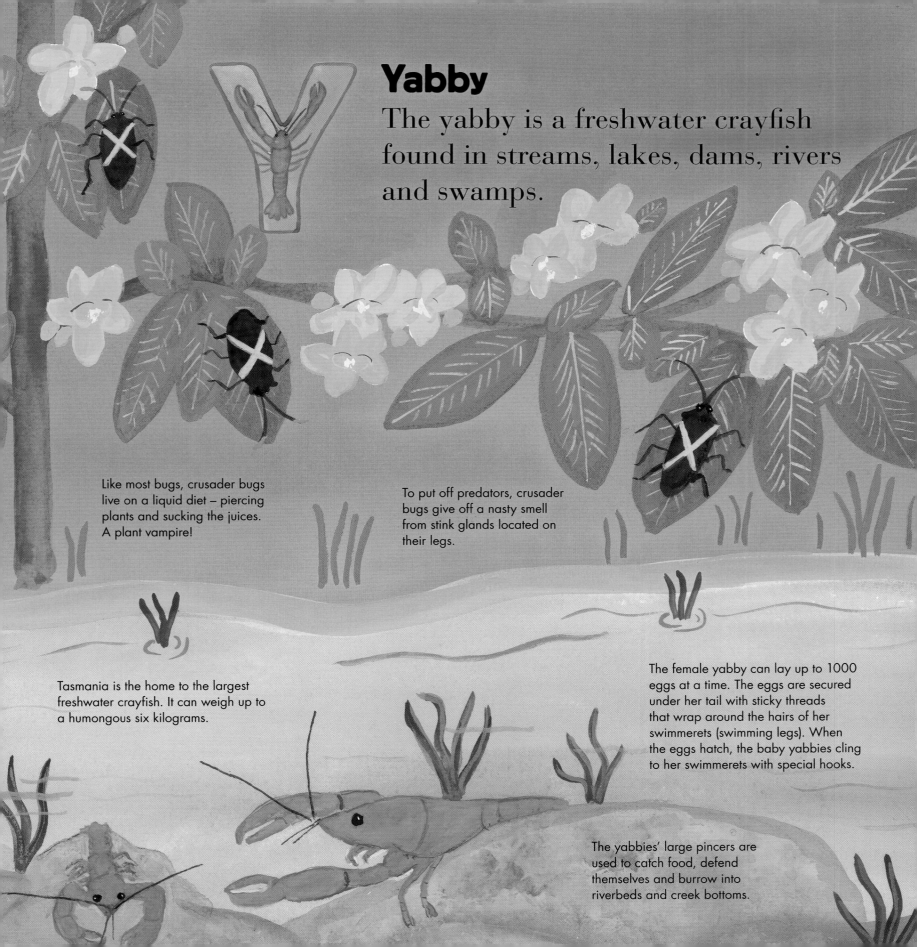

Like most bugs, crusader bugs live on a liquid diet – piercing plants and sucking the juices. A plant vampire!

To put off predators, crusader bugs give off a nasty smell from stink glands located on their legs.

The female yabby can lay up to 1000 eggs at a time. The eggs are secured under her tail with sticky threads that wrap around the hairs of her swimmerets (swimming legs). When the eggs hatch, the baby yabbies cling to her swimmerets with special hooks.

Tasmania is the home to the largest freshwater crayfish. It can weigh up to a humongous six kilograms.

The yabbies' large pincers are used to catch food, defend themselves and burrow into riverbeds and creek bottoms.

Zebra Finch

The zebra finch is a small bird, which lives in large flocks of up to 100 birds or more.

Scientists have discovered that baby zebra finches rehearse and learn to sing songs while they sleep at night.

The black-and-white zebra finch gets its name from the black and white zebra-like stripes on its chest and tail feathers.

For fear that a predator is lurking by a waterhole, zebra finches suck up water quickly, instead of scooping like other birds.

Zebra finches helped save many early explorers from dying of thirst. By following a flock of zebra finches, explorers would eventually be led to water.

During courtship, the male zebra finch performs a solo dance and sings to the female. They remain together for life.

Maps of animal distribution

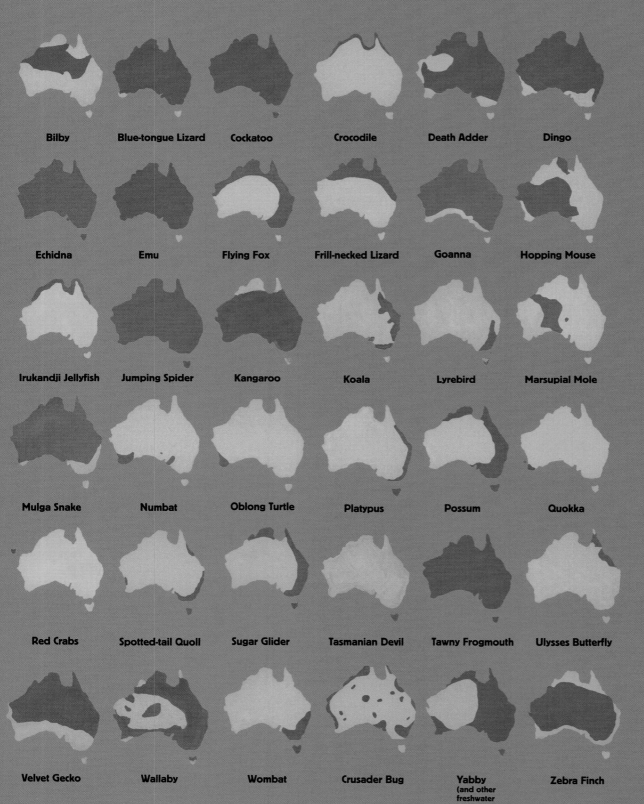

Bilby	Blue-tongue Lizard	Cockatoo
Crocodile	Death Adder	Dingo
Echidna	Emu	Flying Fox
Frill-necked Lizard	Goanna	Hopping Mouse
Irukandji Jellyfish	Jumping Spider	Kangaroo
Koala	Lyrebird	Marsupial Mole
Mulga Snake	Numbat	Oblong Turtle
Platypus	Possum	Quokka
Red Crabs	Spotted-tail Quoll	Sugar Glider
Tasmanian Devil	Tawny Frogmouth	Ulysses Butterfly
Velvet Gecko	Wallaby	Wombat
Crusader Bug	Yabby (and other freshwater crayfish)	Zebra Finch

For my baby animals, Luke and Cody.

Special thanks to Guundie and Gerald Kuching, Nick Mooney, Jürgen Otto, Dr Ken Mulvaney, Wendy Binks and the dream team of Nicola Santilli, Gayna Murphy and Sue Whiting.

First published in 2017
by Walker Books Australia Pty Ltd
Locked Bag 22, Newtown
NSW 2042 Australia
www.walkerbooks.com.au

The moral rights of the author/illustrator
have been asserted.

Text and Illustrations © 2017 Frané Lessac

National Library of Australia
Cataloguing-in-Publication entry:
Lessac, Frané, author, illustrator.
A is for Australian animals / Author/Illustrator Frané Lessac.
ISBN: 978 1 925381 00 9 (hardback)
Subjects: Animals – Australia – Juvenile literature.
591.994

The illustrations for this book were created with gouache
on arches paper
Typeset in Futura Book
Printed and bound in China

3 5 7 9 10 8 6 4 2

FSC
www.fsc.org
MIX
Paper from
responsible sources
FSC® C008047

These maps show the combined distribution of each animal species.

MAP KEY

 Common areas where animal species is found

 Areas where animal species is unlikely or not found